PREPARE YOUR
HEART

A GUIDED ADVENT JOURNAL FOR PRAYER AND MEDITATION

FR. AGUSTINO TORRES, CFR
ILLUSTRATED BY VALERIE DELGADO

AVE MARIA PRESS

Visit our website to find online components, including videos by Fr. Agustino Torres, CFR, to enhance your experience with Prepare Your Heart *this Advent. Go to www.avemaria press.com/private/ page/prepare-your-heart-resources.*

Nihil Obstat: Reverend Monsignor Michael Heintz, PhD
           Censor Librorum
Imprimatur: Most Reverend Kevin C. Rhoades
           Bishop of Fort Wayne–South Bend
Given at: Fort Wayne, Indiana, on 6 March 2023

Founded in 1865, Ave Maria Press is a ministry of the United States Province of Holy Cross.

www.avemariapress.com

Paperback: 978-1-64680-251-7

E-book: 978-1-64680-252-4

Cover and interior images © 2023 Valerie Delgado, paxbeloved.com.

Cover and text design by Brianna Dombo.

Printed and bound in the United States of America.

CONTENTS

INTRODUCTION

We must return to Nazareth in these our times. Not the teeming city of today with its churches built upon ancient edifices and bustling businesses lining the streets; no, the Nazareth of our hearts requires that we go much deeper than the surface. Nazareth, oh town of silence and labor, how we need your eloquent lessons. Nazareth, which saw Joseph and Mary prepare for the birth of our Lord, may we prepare as well. Nazareth, oh hamlet that bore witness to some of the most celebrated events in all of history—the Incarnation, the Annunciation, and the Immaculate Conception—teach us today by calling us deeper.

These feasts that we celebrate in our parishes and communities today did not happen in some abstracted paradise. They occurred on this very earth in a very specific town: Nazareth. This little town in Galilee holds a place in the minds and hearts of Christians around the world. I invite you, too, to enter into Nazareth this Advent.

Let us allow this place to be our teacher as it was witness to Jesus's younger years. The table in the house of the Holy Family nourished our Savior, who nourishes us with the Eucharist. The kitchen in the holy house was tended by the loving hands of the Mother of God. St. Joseph had a workshop in this same place where our Lord learned craftsmanship.

Such marvelous things has this place seen! All this in silent obscurity! These events are not recorded in sacred scripture except for the most essential, but it is here that the Holy Family grew after their return from Egypt. As a mighty oak tree grows without a word, and as a lily blooms, stunning in its stillness, so too was the Holy Family formed in Nazareth.

A FRANCISCAN APPROACH

My brothers and sisters, Franciscan spirituality has dotted the Church calendar with many saints. It is a simple, straightforward spirituality where you enter "by the narrow gate" (Mt 7:13–14). Over the centuries, Franciscans have counted as saints both kings and paupers, queens and former mistresses. We like to call them "saints of the seraphic order."

It is said that Pope Leo XIII toward the end of the nineteenth century surmised, "Should the world grow cold, all that is needed is to revive the spirit of the founder of the Franciscan order." What is this spirit? St. Francis went to Jesus. Our contemporary culture, with its technology and rugged individualism, tends to ask God to enter into our story. By contrast, a Franciscan approach asks God if we can come into his story.

We enter God's story principally by way of prayer, which is meant to lead us to contemplation. Yes, there are many types of prayer, but the ultimate end of prayer is union with God. By this union I do not mean a state of grace but a way of being. It is becoming fully alive by being completely abandoned to him. It is an ascent to the mystical mountain peaks where nothing but God will satisfy. Some have called it the practice of the presence of God or the sacrament of the moment. It is being in a constant state of prayer where God is ours and we are his. It is prayer that is, in many ways, beyond words or images.

Franciscan spirituality calls us to enter into God's story by hearing the words of scripture and then adopting them. St. Francis did this in very simple, direct ways:

✢ He heard the gospel of the rich young man (Mt 19:16–22) and saw that he went away sad for he had many possessions. His heart longed for the Lord to look upon him with love, so he went and sold all he had and gave it to the poor.

✢ St. Francis on Mount Alverna looked upon a crucifix, lamented "love is not loved," and wept, longing to fill up "what is lacking in Christ's afflictions for the sake of his body, that is, the Church" (Col 1:24). Then, in his own body, he saw the wounds of Christ begin to appear during a vision of a seraph angel.

✢ More apt for our meditations herein, St. Francis longed to be in Bethlehem, but he was in the town of Greccio. No matter; with the help of good people, he created the first nativity scene on a hill. The joy of Christ's birth had never been more alive in those who were in attendance.

There is joy that comes from inserting yourself into God's story.

Perhaps you have heard it said, "Keep Christ in Christmas." This, I assure you, can happen if you take a page from the Franciscan way this Advent. Enter into the story. This does require certain commitments from you—prayer, charity to others, and joyful service to the needy. However, the joy of entering into God's story this Advent is not one that can be contained. I invite your family or community to participate in this Advent journey with you; yes, with all the attitudes and complaints, bring your loved ones along. They may not understand at first, but God will bless your perseverance. Let us journey to Nazareth and enter in.

FR. AGUSTINO TORRES

Visit **www.avemariapress.com/private/page/prepare-your-heart-resources** for more information about bulk discounts, a leader's guide, help with organizing a small group, videos from Fr. Agustino Torres, CFR, discussing the theme for each week of Advent, and other resources to help you make the most of your time together with *Prepare Your Heart*.

HOW TO USE THIS JOURNAL

The *Prepare Your Heart* Advent journal's combination of daily meditations, questions for reflection, journaling space, prayers, and beautiful original art is specially designed to draw you into a deeper, richer experience of Advent, preparing you not only to experience the joy of Jesus's birth but also to journey with the saints of this season—especially Joseph and Mary of the Holy Family. We are processing together to the wondrous interruption of history in the birth of our Savior.

WHO IS *PREPARE YOUR HEART* FOR?

Prepare Your Heart is for anyone who desires to experience the Advent season as a journey that draws us into a bigger narrative—one that tells of God's saving work among us. The season of Advent is the ideal time to step back from your life and evaluate where you stand with God, yourself, and others. This Advent journal provides a daily path to prayer and reflection that places our stories in this larger one, where they find purpose and meaning.

Prepare Your Heart is perfect for use in a group setting and was designed with that in mind. There's something special about taking this Advent journey with a community, whether that community is your entire parish, a small group, or your family. You'll find ample suggestions for celebrating the Sundays in Advent in a downloadable at **www.avemariapress.com/private/page/prepare-your-heart-resources**. Included are ideas for meals, songs, prayers, and crafts throughout the

Advent season. Visit **www.avemariapress.com/private/page/ prepare-your-heart-resources** for more information about bulk discounts, a leader's guide, help with organizing a small group, videos from Fr. Agustino Torres discussing the theme for each week of Advent, and other resources to help you make the most of your time together with *Prepare Your Heart*.

You can also use *Prepare Your Heart* strictly as an individual, with the meditations and journaling prompts helping you draw near to God, hear his voice in new ways, and pour out your heart to him as your turn your attention to the example of the Holy Family. You may find that this Advent you're in special need of regular, quiet times of connection with God; *Prepare Your Heart* is an excellent way to help you find that space each day.

HOW IS *PREPARE YOUR HEART* ORGANIZED?

Prepare Your Heart is organized into four parts:

✤ The first part turns your attention to the Holy Family's life in Nazareth.

✤ In the second part you'll learn more about the saints of this Advent season—the figures that the Church in her wisdom places before us as we prepare for Christmas: Mary, St. John the Baptist, St. Lucy, St. Nicholas, St. Andrew, St. Juan Diego, and Our Lady of Guadalupe.

✤ The third part leads you to reflect on the virtues of St. Joseph: his silent yes, his creative courage, and his humility, gentleness, joy, and prayerfulness. We look to his example and intercession to build a home within us where the Holy Family can dwell, just as he built their home in Nazareth.

✦ In the final week of Advent, as Christmas draws near, we turn our attention to Mary, reflecting on her virtues and example to help us create space within us for Christ to be born. We will look at Mary's prayerfulness, her willingness to say yes, and her trust.

Within each week, you'll encounter a simple daily pattern made up of the following parts:

✦ Each day opens with an excerpt from scripture, the *Catechism*, or trusted voices meant to focus your thoughts on the key idea from that day's meditation. Try to pray with the excerpt in silence while listening to what word or phrase jumps out at you.

✦ The *meditation* from Fr. Torres draws out a message from the season of Advent, scripture, saints, or Franciscan spirituality.

✦ The *reflect* section challenges you to ponder and journal in response to the meditation, helping you identify practical ways to live out the Advent season more fully.

✦ Finally, after you've read and journaled, the closing *prayer* provides a starting point for your own requests and prayers of thanksgiving and praise to God.

HOW SHOULD I READ
PREPARE YOUR HEART?

This Advent journal's daily format is flexible enough to accommodate any reader's preferences. If you're a morning person, you may want to start your day with *Prepare Your Heart*, completing the entire day's reading, reflection, journaling, and prayer first thing in the morning. Or you may find that you prefer to end your day by using *Prepare Your Heart* to focus your attention on God as you begin to rest from the day's activities. You may even decide to read and pray as a family in the morning and journal individually in the evening.

The key is finding what works for you, ensuring that you have time to read carefully, ponder deeply, write honestly, and connect intimately with the Lord in prayer.

Whatever approach you choose (and whether you decide to experience *Prepare Your Heart* with a group or on your own), be sure to visit **www.avemariapress.com/private/page/ prepare-your-heart-resources** for extra resources to help you get the most out of this special Advent journey.

FIRST WEEK OF ADVENT
THE WAY OF NAZARETH

FIRST WEEK OF ADVENT

SUNDAY

AND [JESUS] WENT DOWN WITH
THEM AND CAME TO NAZARETH,
AND WAS OBEDIENT TO THEM;
AND HIS MOTHER KEPT ALL
THESE THINGS IN HER HEART.
AND JESUS INCREASED IN
WISDOM AND IN STATURE, AND
IN FAVOR WITH GOD AND MAN.

LUKE 2:51–52

A HOME IN NAZARETH

Although Advent is a time of joyful anticipation, it is also a time when we can do some penance and order our hearts to prepare the way for the coming Christ child. What I call living a Gospel-centered life, St. Francis would call "the way of penance." Advent is not penitential in the same way Lent is, but there has been a long-held tradition in the Church to offer up prayer vigils, fasts, and offerings during Advent. I suggest you begin this Advent by *responding to God* through prayer and fasting. Choose what daily habit you will begin or daily sacrifice you will make for the next four weeks, and be intentional about sticking to it.

As we begin the first week of preparation for the Christmas feast, I invite you to join me in the school of Nazareth. Throughout Advent, we'll be studying the followers of Christ—the saints—as well as Joseph and Mary. We will see many good examples of humility, joy, and trust, but now it is time to visit the Holy Family and make ourselves at home with them in Nazareth.

Nazareth is a place where just enough rain falls for some growth. This is the norm of our own spiritual growth—there is just enough to keep on going. We would prefer to swim in consolation, and we often feel like something is wrong when we do not experience it. Yet most of our spiritual growth occurs in desolation or just on the border of it. This is Nazareth. Here Jesus can grow. It is rare that in the light one can see the stars. The sun must set so that we may see what lies beyond.

By contemplating Nazareth, we create space where our hearts can become Jesus's home. Jesus will increase within us and grow in stature if we walk alongside him in Nazareth and live in obedience. There is a freedom in knowing that, in being subject to proper authority, we are free. Though the winds of the world batter against this age-old secret of spiritual growth, it is in the quiet, ordinary humility of Nazareth where we are allowed to see the stars in the night.

We do not experience the dark for the sake of darkness. We do not feel desolate for the sake of desolation. These are opportunities for Christ to grow in us. For it is in this darkness and desolation that we exercise the life of faith, grow in knowing who God is and who we are, and grow detached from things that are ultimately unnecessary.

REFLECT

1. What is it that hinders your heart from growing in union with God?
2. What can you learn from the school of Nazareth about the ebbs and flows of the spiritual life?

PRAY

*HELP ME, LORD, TO HOLD FAST. THE
TRAGEDIES SEEM TO MOUNT, AND
THE UNCERTAINTIES ARE RISING TO
MY NECK. THERE IS A LONELINESS
IN FOLLOWING YOU. GRANT ME THE
GRACE TO ACCEPT THIS. GRANT ME
THE GRACE TO BE OBEDIENT TO YOUR
WORD. GRANT ME THE GRACE TO SEE
LIGHT IN THE DARKNESS AND HEAR
SINGING IN THE SILENCE.*

FIRST WEEK OF ADVENT

MONDAY

NATHAN'A-EL SAID TO HIM, "CAN
ANYTHING GOOD COME OUT
OF NAZARETH?" PHILIP SAID TO
HIM, "COME AND SEE."

JOHN 1:46

THE LITTLE PLACE

Can anything good come from Nazareth? This was the question of Nathaniel when he was about to meet Jesus. Let us consider the call of this little town. Nazareth was not wise according to human standards; Athens would have been chosen for this. Nor was it a powerful center of military might; Rome would have done well here. Nor was it of noble birth; Jerusalem would have made more sense. So then, why Nazareth? Why, of all places on God's creation, was this town chosen for the place where Jesus would be raised?

The *Catechism* reminds us that "during the greater part of his life, Jesus shared the condition of the vast majority of human beings: a daily life spent without evident greatness, a life of manual labor" (531). In Nazareth, Jesus was able to experience the ordinary drudgery of a hidden life, the same kind of life most of us experience.

You are Nazareth. You, oh little soul longing to grow closer to God, are like this place. Perhaps you do not have the highest learning by human standards. Perhaps you are not the strongest or the most noble. It is precisely by acknowledging that you are little that the Lord can grow within you as he did in a little place.

Can anything good come out of a little place like Nazareth? A little place like your own neighborhood? A little place like your own family with its quirks, with its brokenness and disappointments? A little place like your school or workplace, where you seem to toil without end toward a goal that is hard to see? Can anything good come out of little places like these?

If we join the disciples and follow Jesus the Nazarene, we will see.

REFLECT

1. In what ways do you experience feeling little?
2. How can you offer the little, everyday occurrences in union with Mary and Joseph in Nazareth and remain with them in the presence of Jesus?

PRAY

LORD, I WILL FOLLOW EVEN IF I FEEL LIKE A FAILURE. I WILL FOLLOW EVEN IF IT SEEMS THAT I'M NOT DOING IT RIGHT. YOUR PRESENCE, LORD, IS MY FREEDOM. THOUGH ALL AROUND ME COVER ME WITH PRAISE, IT DOES NOT SATISFY MY HEART. THOUGH MANY MAY SHARE FLATTERING WORDS, IT IS NOT THIS THAT CAN SUSTAIN ME, BUT ONLY SAY A WORD AND YOUR SERVANT SHALL BE HEALED. YES, LORD, SAY THE WORD. LET YOUR WILL BE DONE IN ME. GRANT ME THE GRACE TO LOVE YOUR WILL.

FIRST WEEK OF ADVENT

TUESDAY

MAY NAZARETH TEACH US THE
MEANING OF FAMILY LIFE,
ITS HARMONY OF LOVE, ITS
SIMPLICITY AND AUSTERE
BEAUTY, ITS SACRED AND
INVIOLABLE CHARACTER.

POPE PAUL VI

PART OF THE FAMILY

There is joy and peace in Nazareth. Just imagine with me some of the daily scenes there. Place yourself as a visitor in the home of the Holy Family, and watch, listen, taste, smell, and feel what it is like.

Hear St. Joseph, the craftsman, putting his tools down and walking in the door after a long day of labor. He is moving slowly, but savoring the silent joy of returning home, hands worn and body tired. You can smell the sweet aroma of Our Lady's meals throughout the house.

Sit next to Joseph at their meal at the middle of the day; to partake of the wisdom shared at the table in Nazareth can make our souls glad. Listen to the conversation, the thoughtful exchanges, their heartfelt humor. See Jesus and Mary glance at each other with a smile when Joseph tells the same story again. He knows they've heard it before, but it's a good story. Joseph looks at you, too. Without saying anything, you exchange a knowing look. This is the joy of being seen and being known.

Imagine a different time of day with sunlight streaming in a window. The lady of the house is singing a song. The words speak of comfort. The melody reassures you of her presence and communicates love. Your fears melt away. In some way, the song reminds you of a much bigger story we are part of, one that puts into perspective the problems you face and the questions you have. The emotions that once suffocated you have no response to the simple tune. Anxiety relaxes its grip, and everything silently finds its rightful place within you.

What are the words that you hear in this sweet song? She is standing over you, and you are in her shadow, under her protection. Do you feel joy welling up within your heart? You are safe and set free. You are in the hollow of her mantle and in the crossing of her arms. Do you need anything more?

REFLECT

1. What is it like to spend time with Joseph and Mary in their home in Nazareth? What emotions come up for you?
2. What would you like to say to Joseph or Mary? What do you ask of them?

PRAY

LORD JESUS, JOIN ME AS I IMAGINE
YOUR HOME LIFE. SPEND TIME WITH
ME AS I SPEND TIME WITH YOUR
MOM AND DAD. IN COMING TO
KNOW THEM BETTER, I AM COMING
TO KNOW YOU BETTER, TOO. HELP
ME HAVE CONFIDENCE THAT I AM
A GOOD FRIEND OF YOUR FAMILY,
SOMEONE WHO CAN WALK IN WITHOUT
KNOCKING, SOMEONE WHO ALWAYS
HAS A PLACE AT THE DINNER TABLE.
HELP ME FEEL AT HOME WITH YOU.

FIRST WEEK OF ADVENT

WEDNESDAY

LORD, THAT I MIGHT NOT BE
PROUD, THAT I MIGHT NOT BE
SELF-SUFFICIENT, THAT I MIGHT
NOT BELIEVE THAT I AM THE
CENTER OF THE UNIVERSE. MAKE
ME HUMBLE. GRANT ME THE
GRACE OF HUMILITY. AND WITH
THIS HUMILITY, MAY I FIND YOU.
IT IS THE ONLY WAY; WITHOUT
HUMILITY WE WILL NEVER FIND
GOD: WE WILL FIND OURSELVES.

POPE FRANCIS

LOVE IN THE ORDINARY

I was invited to hear confessions at a Carmelite monastery a while back. The mother superior wanted to speak to me beforehand and give me an orientation. To be honest, I did not think it was necessary. What possible sins could these sisters have experienced closed up in a cloister? "Sanctification occurs in the ordinary," the mother superior told me. "Perhaps you will not hear great sins from the sisters, but holiness grows through everyday things."

Nazareth held on to a secret for many years. A great healing was being prepared for the whole world. How the people of Israel waited for the messiah, the anointed one, the one who would save us! The salvation that was planned was far greater than freeing any earthly kingdom from oppression. This salvation was meant for not only one nation but the entire world. How great is God that he would show his power beyond what anyone could imagine.

Nazareth held this secret in plain sight. The Savior of the world was familiar to the townspeople there. When he returned to preach the coming of the kingdom, they rejected him because they could not believe that one of them could be the chosen one.

He comes to us, too, in our everyday experiences. In the ordinary parts of our lives, God's salvation is fulfilled in our hearing, yet we turn away from his love. Now is the time to turn again to him. Today is the day of salvation. We are redeemed by his offering of his own life. Be at peace, but do not delay any longer.

REFLECT

1. What parts of your life seem too simple or familiar for God to enter in and use for your salvation? Whom might you reject or dismiss because they are too ordinary?
2. How can you listen more deeply for God's word throughout your day today?

PRAY

*LORD, LOVE HAS BEEN FORMED
IN ME AS AN IDEA, A SENSATION,
A MOUNTAIN TOP, A GLORIOUS
TRIUMPH. I GET INVESTED IN AND
DISTRACTED BY MY EMOTIONS,
PLEASURE, AND EXPECTATIONS. MAY
THE WAY OF NAZARETH TEACH ME HOW
LOVE IS GLORIOUS, INDEED, BUT ALSO
MONOTONOUS AND MUNDANE. MAY IT
TEACH ME HOW AFFECTION IS REGULAR
AND REPETITIVE. HELP ME ADJUST
MY VISION SO THAT I CAN FIND YOU
REACHING FOR ME HERE AND NOW IN
THE EVERYDAY PARTS OF MY LIFE.*

FIRST WEEK OF ADVENT
THURSDAY

AND HE ROSE AND TOOK THE
CHILD AND HIS MOTHER,
AND WENT TO THE LAND OF
ISRAEL. . . . AND HE WENT
AND DWELT IN A CITY CALLED
NAZARETH, THAT WHAT WAS
SPOKEN BY THE PROPHETS MIGHT
BE FULFILLED, "HE SHALL BE
CALLED A NAZARENE."

MATTHEW 2:21–23

ONE STEP AT A TIME

The distance from Joachim and Anne's home to that of Joseph and Mary's in Nazareth was a few thousand feet up a hill. We know Joseph was a skilled worker. We can imagine that he contributed to the building of the holy house of Nazareth.

After Joseph's dream he took into his home Mary, a pregnant girl in her teens (Mt 1:24). Let us ask for entrance into this house. Did our Blessed Mother ask Joseph to build them a house on a hill in Nazareth so they could be close to her parents? For the sake of our contemplation, let us enter into that scene. Let us assist in carrying the stones as Joseph gives us instruction and bringing in the food at Mary's sweet command.

As we place the stones next to Joseph, as we envision Mary describing the size of the room she wants for the baby, we can see their plans and hopes taking shape. They didn't know how their story was going to proceed or how it would end. All they knew is that they were given a special task from God. They gave their best effort to care for that gift, to give Jesus a home. They knew God would take care of the rest. They could only ever see one step ahead of them, but they took it in faith, and God showed them the next step.

We can practice this faithfulness, too. We can trust God as Joseph and Mary did by listening well to what God is asking of us in the here and now. We can build a home for the Lord—a space in our hearts where he can dwell with us. When it's time to take the next step, God will tell us where to go.

REFLECT

1. When do you feel most restless about your life? What distractions do you look for to fill up this restlessness?
2. How can you turn this restlessness into quiet acts of prayer and service that grow faith?

PRAY

*SEND ME, LORD. SEND ME AND
I WILL GO. HELP ME TO UNDERSTAND
YOUR CALL. TO KNOW I AM CALLED
TO BE WITH YOU. TO ENTER INTO THE
CHAMBER OF YOUR LOVE AND NOT
BE AFRAID OF REJECTION. TO KNOW
THAT YOU ARE DESIROUS OF MY SOUL.
YOU, LIKE A LOVER, PURSUE MY HEART.
WHAT IS IT, LORD, THAT MAKES YOU
SO DESIRE ME? HOW CAN I, POOR
SINNER, BE SO LOVED BY SO
GREAT A GOD?*

FIRST WEEK OF ADVENT

FRIDAY

WE DON'T HAVE THE ANSWERS,
BUT WE KNOW THAT JESUS
SUFFERED JUST LIKE YOU,
BECAUSE HE TOO WAS
INNOCENT. THE TRUE GOD WHO
COMES TO LIFE IN JESUS IS WITH
US. EVEN IN SADNESS, WHEN WE
DON'T HAVE ALL THE ANSWERS,
GOD IS ON OUR SIDE AND THAT
WILL HELP US.

POPE BENEDICT XVI

HIDDEN CROSSES

During Advent Franciscans often hold vigil prayers during the night to encourage us to wait on the Lord. At times, we will gather in the middle of the night by candlelight for our early morning prayer. One year I was so sleepy I decided to pray on my knees to stay awake. When it was my turn to lead the prayers, I meant in my mind to say the prayer but what came out of my mouth was, "Sleeeep." My brothers all broke out into laughter, even at that early hour of the morning.

The sacrifice of a vigil is a small way we participate in the cross. Some crosses are public and easy to see. Sometimes we suffer in ways that draw a lot of attention. Most of the crosses we bear, though, are quiet and hidden. Jesus knew both of these crosses.

The Romans purposefully crucified people near the gate of Jerusalem for maximum visibility. That's why they killed Jesus there. Jesus carried many crosses in Nazareth, too, but there they were crosses no one could see. He labored with Joseph, but despite all their sweat, no one remembers what they built. He observed small-town gossip and watched people mistreat each other. He was subject to a political system that only seemed to keep wealth at the top and everyone else in their place—and he had to pay taxes to support it. He saw people wonder if there was more to life than getting up every day to work to the point of exhaustion.

In Jerusalem, Jesus was ridiculed and rejected for our salvation, but in Nazareth, he would practice the way of nothingness, hidden in ordinary life.

Following the way of Nazareth allows us to take up whatever crosses come to us in the small and hidden parts of our lives. In bearing them well with courage, patience, and faith, we are preparing to follow Jesus through death to life.

REFLECT

1. What is a small, hidden cross you are invited to bear, one that no one else can see? How can you carry it with faith?
2. Who in your life is bearing a cross right now? How can you help them carry it?

PRAY

LORD, RECEIVE MY BROKENNESS.
THERE ARE THINGS I CANNOT CHANGE,
MEMORIES THAT DO NOT FADE AWAY.
HEAR MY CRY AND LISTEN TO MY NEED.
THE ANXIETIES OF LIFE SURROUND ME
LIKE A CLOUD. MY FAILURES HAUNT
ME. YET EVEN THIS CAN SANCTIFY ME
IF I FOLLOW THE WAY OF NAZARETH
AND LEARN TO CARRY MY CROSS.
THERE IS NO CROSS THAT CANNOT BE
REDEEMED. GRANT ME FAITH TO SEE
YOUR PATIENT WORK WITHIN ME.

FIRST WEEK OF ADVENT

SATURDAY

BY HIS OBEDIENCE TO MARY
AND JOSEPH, AS WELL AS BY
HIS HUMBLE WORK DURING
THE LONG YEARS IN NAZARETH,
JESUS GIVES US THE EXAMPLE
OF HOLINESS IN THE DAILY LIFE
OF FAMILY AND WORK.

*CATECHISM OF THE CATHOLIC
CHURCH 564*

LISTEN AND LEARN

Jesus went to Nazareth and was obedient to his parents—imagine that! The divine incarnation of the Word of God being obedient to mere human beings. Mary asked him to do chores around the house. Joseph asked him to carry beams at the work site. Jesus obeyed them.

The root of the word *obey* is "to hear." Look at the extreme humility of God, that he who is almighty would listen to his own creation. In his divinity, Jesus knew all things. But in his humanity, he learned how to read, how to build, how to love. He learned in Nazareth.

What can I learn from the school of Nazareth about being obedient? How can I be like Jesus in this way? He did not declare his divine authority to his parents. No, he was obedient. Obedience is the proof of holiness. We, too, must be obedient and trust in God's promise never to abandon us.

The Lord is on his way. He is coming to save us. What a joy to ponder that his salvation will set us free. No more crying, no more pain. We have wandered far. Our lives are filled with blessings, but there is also loss and bitterness that can be difficult to endure. The Lord is our deliverer who stands by to lift these burdens and set our feet aright. What wonderful news! What a glorious God we serve! Our response is needed, and we should make every effort to draw nearer.

Our response is not an unthinking obedience, but rather like Joseph, that we be transformed by the renewal of our minds (cf. Romans 12:2). To be obedient is to unite our wills to God's will—that we do what we know is right, even if it is not easy or convenient. God has spoken his Word. It is up to us to hear it and to change our lives.

REFLECT

1. What can you learn from the school of Nazareth about being obedient? How can you be more like Jesus in this area?
2. How can you listen for God's will? In what areas can you be more humble or obedient?

_____

_____

_____

_____

_____

PRAY

OH LORD, HOW OFTEN I TALK TO YOU WITHOUT LISTENING. I COME TO YOU FULL OF MY NEEDS AND WORRIES. I GO ON AND ON ABOUT WHAT IS HAPPENING IN MY LIFE. HELP ME MAKE ROOM TO LISTEN TO YOU— TO TAKE ON SILENCE, TO GO FOR A WALK WITHOUT ANY DISTRACTIONS, TO HEAR YOU IN MY OWN BREATHING. IN LISTENING TO YOU, MAY I BECOME OBEDIENT TO YOU, TO FOLLOW WHERE YOU ARE PULLING MY HEART. YOU LISTENED TO JOSEPH AND MARY IN OBEDIENCE; HELP ME LISTEN TO YOU IN OBEDIENCE, TOO.

SECOND WEEK
OF ADVENT
THE WAY OF
THE SAINTS

SECOND WEEK OF ADVENT

SUNDAY

THE ANGEL GABRIEL WAS SENT
FROM GOD TO A CITY OF
GALILEE NAMED NAZARETH,
TO A VIRGIN BETROTHED TO A
MAN WHOSE NAME WAS JOSEPH,
OF THE HOUSE OF DAVID; AND
THE VIRGIN'S NAME WAS MARY.
AND HE CAME TO HER AND
SAID, "HAIL, FULL OF GRACE,
THE LORD IS WITH YOU!" BUT
SHE WAS GREATLY TROUBLED AT
THE SAYING, AND CONSIDERED
IN HER MIND WHAT SORT OF
GREETING THIS MIGHT BE.

LUKE 1:26–29

AN INTENTIONAL RESPONSE

As we journey through Advent with the Holy Family in Nazareth, we are accompanied by the host of angels and saints in the Church. Each and every single one of us has a purpose—a calling. Ultimately, we are all called to be holy, and whatever our perception of that word is, the saints can be teachers that help make that more approachable. We will focus this week on seven key figures: Mary of Nazareth, John the Baptist, Andrew of Galilee, Nicholas of Smyrna, Lucy of Rome, Juan Diego Cuauhtlatoatzin, and Our Lady of Guadalupe. These saints each have something to teach us about the bold humility that we find in the small town of Nazareth.

If we were to look for what makes the saints holy, we'd quickly land on the idea that every one of them responded to God. God spoke to them, and they responded *with intention.*

We see this intentionality so clearly in the life of Mary of Nazareth, who was a young, Jewish girl when the angel Gabriel announced to her that she would be the mother of our Savior. We know from the Gospel of Luke that Mary asked a very important question to the angel, "How can this be when I have had no relations with a man?" The answer that was given was not a detailed, step-by-step guide, but she trusted and gave her fiat: "Behold, I am the handmaid of the Lord; let it be to me according to your word" (Lk 1:38). In this response, she opens herself to God's power, and we all know how that story unfolds.

In our own lives, we can easily begin to feel like God is silent, like he's not even there. These can be times when it becomes necessary for us to take the first step, to respond to God by being intentional in what we *do.* Because our actions affect our thoughts, we must search ourselves to learn what actions will best help us recognize God all around us and what choices will foster an attitude of faith and trust in God.

REFLECT

1. How has God spoken to you in the past? In what relationships, events, prayer habits, or moments can you see God's power in your life?
2. What can you do to simplify your life this Advent? What can you give up in a spirit of penance and vigil?

_____

_____

_____

_____

_____

_____

_____

_____

_____

PRAY

LORD, PLACE IN ME A CLEAN HEART.
ALLOW YOUR PLAN FOR ME TO TAKE
HOLD OF MY HEART, AND LET ME
NOT TURN AWAY. HOW PATIENT YOU
ARE WITH YOUR CHILDREN. AFTER SO
MANY GIFTS OF GOLD, WE TURN BACK
TO MUD AND GRIME. AFTER BEING
CLEANED UP IN YOUR MERCY, WE
WANDER. TAKE ME BACK AGAIN, OH
LORD, TAKE ME BACK.

35

SECOND WEEK OF ADVENT

MONDAY

THERE WAS A MAN SENT FROM
GOD, WHOSE NAME WAS JOHN.
HE CAME FOR TESTIMONY, TO
BEAR WITNESS TO THE LIGHT,
THAT ALL MIGHT BELIEVE
THROUGH HIM. HE WAS NOT
THE LIGHT, BUT CAME TO BEAR
WITNESS TO THE LIGHT.

JOHN 1:6-8

SEE AND BELIEVE

As we peer into the life of John the Baptist today, we find another dimension of our response to God. John can teach us how to identify God in the midst of our everyday lives and make that light known to those around us. The scriptures tell us that John begins his important work before he's even born. When pregnant Mary visits Elizabeth, John leaps in Elizabeth's womb, signaling his recognition of his Savior's presence and leading Elizabeth to announce Mary's blessedness. We can even look back to David dancing before the ark and see how he foreshadowed John the Baptist dancing in the womb at the presence of God in the womb of Mary.

Of course, it's then John who baptizes Jesus, leading God the Father to proclaim from heaven, "This is my beloved Son, with whom I am well pleased" (Mt 3:17). Even today, baptism is the first sacrament each Christian receives. Another moment when John is the first to see Jesus is found in the Gospel of John, when he says, "Behold, the Lamb of God" (1:29). Here, he is telling his two disciples to do, for the first time, what he has done before them: to see and believe. We hear this proclaimed at every Mass during the Liturgy of the Eucharist. The priest repeats John's words while raising the host because we are to do what John did: to see and believe as if it's the first time, every time.

In other words, *we have to go for it*. There is a gift in beholding the Lamb of God, but many times it is lost among distractions and preoccupations. Heaven is being opened to us, but we must take the step to receive it. Again, we turn to the words of John the Baptist, who says, "He must increase, but I must decrease" (Jn 3:30). To do this, we must have hearts that are open to the love God wants to give us, and then respond by sharing this love with others. We will most easily find him in the disguise of the poor and brokenhearted around us. May we show love to those in need and help heal any wounds we have caused when our hearts were not directed by God.

REFLECT

1. How is God calling you to decrease so that he might increase in your life?
2. In what ways can you be the "first" to show God's love to others?

_____

_____

_____

_____

_____

_____

_____

_____

PRAY

LORD, PREPARE THE WAY IN MY HEART.
ALLOW MY HEART TO SEE YOU AND BE
READY TO RECEIVE YOU WHEN YOU
COME IN GLORY. HELP ME HUNGER
FOR THE BANQUET OF HEAVEN. PLACE
IN MY HEART A FIRE TO GO TO THE
HIGHWAYS AND BYWAYS TO INVITE ALL
WHO WOULD COME ALONG. HAVE YOUR
WAY IN MY HEART. HEAR MY PRAYERS
FOR MY LOVED ONES: MAY THEY DRAW
NEARER TO YOU.

SECOND WEEK OF ADVENT

TUESDAY

AS HE WALKED BY THE SEA
OF GALILEE, HE SAW TWO
BROTHERS, SIMON WHO IS
CALLED PETER AND ANDREW
HIS BROTHER, CASTING A NET
INTO THE SEA; FOR THEY WERE
FISHERMEN. AND HE SAID TO
THEM, "FOLLOW ME, AND I WILL
MAKE YOU FISHERS OF MEN."
IMMEDIATELY THEY LEFT THEIR
NETS AND FOLLOWED HIM.

MATTHEW 4:18-20

THE HIDDEN WORK

Like his brother Peter, Andrew was a fisherman in Galilee. In the Gospel of John, we read that Andrew was the first to be called by Christ to become an apostle. In the Byzantine church he received a title, *Protokletos,* the first to be called, but he also said yes to Jesus's radical call. The gospels share how Andrew was able to respond to God and invite others to follow as well.

Likely due to his trading activity in the markets of Galilee, Andrew was adept at networking and connecting people to resources, essential skills in the work of evangelization. He told his brother Peter about the messiah and made the meeting happen (Jn 1:41). Later, when all the apostles threw their hands up at the prospect of feeding five thousand men, Andrew brought forward a young boy who had five loaves and two fish (Jn 6:8–9)—I cannot help but imagine this young boy as being wonderfully plump. When some Greeks wanted to meet Jesus, they approached Phillip, but Phillip went to Andrew to arrange the meeting (Jn 12:20–22).

We all know a person like Andrew. The colleague who calls us up just to tell us that they just ate at an amazing restaurant and thought of us. The friend who remembers to send cards at Christmas and on our birthday. The family member who is always happy to see you or never forgets to scratch out a thank-you note. The person who is so thoughtful in connecting us with others with similar interests. It doesn't take much to recognize that these gestures are yet additional forms of authentic intentionality and can be part of our response to God.

This sort of work is quiet and, in some ways, hidden. No one ever became famous for writing a thank-you note or making an introduction. Andrew himself is not an apostle that we discuss often. But does that make him matter any less? Of course not.

He worked tirelessly, strategically, and subtly, drawing on his God-given gifts along the way.

The village of Nazareth calls us to a similar style and mission: give your radical *yes* to Jesus, notice opportunities to do his work within the circumstances of your daily life, and draw on your gifts to enable you. Let us pray for a little bit of the grace Andrew had to tirelessly bring good people together for the glory of God.

REFLECT

1. What are the areas in your life where you can bring people together for the glory of God in your workplace, family, friendships, and community of faith?
2. In what way can you say yes to God today? What skills has he given you to further his kingdom?

PRAY

*OH JESUS, PREPARE MY HEART FOR
GREATER DEPTH SO THAT I CAN SAY
YES TO YOUR CALL FOR ME. THANK
YOU FOR ALL THE PEOPLE YOU HAVE
SENT ME TO BRING ME CLOSER TO
YOU. HELP ME TO LOVE AND SERVE
THEM WELL. HEAR THEIR PETITIONS
AND BLESS THEM.*

SECOND WEEK OF ADVENT

WEDNESDAY

IS NOT THIS THE FAST THAT I CHOOSE:
TO LOOSE THE BONDS OF WICKEDNESS,
TO UNDO THE THONGS OF THE YOKE,
TO LET THE OPPRESSED GO FREE, AND
TO BREAK EVERY YOKE?

IS IT NOT TO SHARE YOUR BREAD
WITH THE HUNGRY, AND BRING THE
HOMELESS POOR INTO YOUR HOUSE;
WHEN YOU SEE THE NAKED, TO COVER
HIM, AND NOT TO HIDE YOURSELF
FROM YOUR OWN FLESH?

THEN SHALL YOUR LIGHT BREAK FORTH
LIKE THE DAWN. . . . THEN YOU SHALL
CALL, AND THE LORD WILL ANSWER;
YOU SHALL CRY, AND HE WILL SAY,
HERE I AM.

ISAIAH 58:6-9

POVERTY CHECK

St. Nicholas has a special place in the Advent and Christmas season. He is well known as Santa Claus, a name derived from the Dutch name *Sinterklaus*. He was a bishop in the town of Myra in modern-day Turkey during the time of the Roman Empire. He heard the plight of a family that had come upon hard times and whose father was going to give his three daughters away to prostitution. Nicholas got wind of this and on successive nights threw bags of gold into their house—first through the window, then down the chimney, and then in the stockings that were hung out to dry. He is reported to have performed miracles, especially those of healing. Perhaps there is a connection between hearing of people's difficulties, alleviating poverty, and healing.

In the friary, we have something we call a poverty check. It is a time when we examine the way we are living on a practical level and do away with things that we haven't used or don't need. We do this four times a year, and one of those falls around Advent. Much more than a fall cleaning, it is a time to take seriously our vow of poverty and live it out.

One danger of our consumer culture is the unnecessary accumulation of material things. I invite you to ponder your own call to live the evangelical counsel of poverty according to your state in life. How can you truly simplify? There is a need for perspective. Let us go out to our little brothers and sisters, the poor, so that we may learn from them.

December has by now caught up to busy homes. By now the plans are in place or are being set for Christmas parties and visits among family. Let us not forget people who are poor and look for Jesus among them. Let us, like St. Nicholas, assist those who have come under hard times, and God will bring about the healing.

1. How can you be more generous with those who are materially impoverished or are poor of heart?
2. How has this past year shown you your own poverty of heart?

_____

_____

_____

_____

_____

_____

_____

_____

_____

_____

_____

_____

_____

_____

PRAY

LORD, GRANT ME A LOVE FOR THE
POOR. I DO NOT WANT TO SERVE
FOR PITY; DELIVER ME FROM GIVING
OUT OF SELFISHNESS. GRANT ME THE
GRACE TO SEE YOUR FACE IN THOSE
WHO BEFORE WERE INVISIBLE TO ME.
ALLOW ME TO LOOK UP TO IN LOVE AT
THOSE WHOM I LOOKED DOWN UPON
IN THE PAST. IF I HAVE GIVEN MORE
FOR MY OWN SAKE THAN FOR YOURS, I
PRAY THAT YOU RECEIVE ALL MY POOR
HEART CAN GIVE, BUT DO NOT ALLOW
ME TO STAY THERE. GIVE ME A HEART
BURNING WITH LOVE FOR YOUR
LITTLE ONES.

SECOND WEEK OF ADVENT

THURSDAY

FOR ONCE YOU WERE DARKNESS,
BUT NOW YOU ARE LIGHT IN THE
LORD; WALK AS CHILDREN OF
LIGHT (FOR THE FRUIT OF LIGHT
IS FOUND IN ALL THAT IS GOOD
AND RIGHT AND TRUE).

EPHESIANS 5:8–9

LIVE IN THE LIGHT

St. Lucy, whose feast day is December 13, is another one of our Advent companions. Lucy was a martyr of the early Church, and while much of her story is shrouded in legend, we do know that she lost her life during the bloody persecution of Christians in the early fourth century. At that time, the Roman emperor Diocletian was merciless in how he killed the Christians; he had them burned, stabbed, beheaded, and tortured to death. We can be sure that however Lucy died was by brutal means. She must have possessed exceptional courage in refusing to renounce her Christian faith.

Because she was a young woman at the time, she has become regarded as a saint who can teach us about the qualities of a childlike faith and what it means to be a light in the darkness. She loved Jesus and believed with her whole heart that he was God, the ultimate lover and possessor of her soul. In her bravery, she bore this truth to others and was met with martyrdom.

We might think of martyrdom as a thing of the past, but the truth is that Christians are ruthlessly murdered every day in the modern world. In lands far and near, those who believe in Jesus live in daily fear of losing their lives or the lives of their loved ones. Like Lucy, these contemporary martyrs profess the same creed you and I do—that Jesus Christ is fully God and fully man, that he came to save us all from sin and bring us into heaven with him. May we remember the global Church today, and may we seek to bear the light of truth to others in the context of our everyday lives.

1. Who has been a bearer of light in your life? How did they impact you?
2. How can you bring light into someone else's life?

PRAY

JESUS, YOU DESIRE THE HEALING OF
THE WORLD THIS ADVENT. IN ORDER
FOR THERE TO BE PEACE ON EARTH, IT
MUST BEGIN IN MY OWN HEART, WHICH
YOU DESIRE ENTIRELY. HELP ME TO SEE
HOW I CAN BRAVELY GIVE MYSELF TO
YOU AND TO THOSE AROUND ME. HELP
ME TO BE A LIGHT IN THIS WORLD AND
TO SHARE THE JOY OF MY FAITH
WITH OTHERS.

51

SECOND WEEK OF ADVENT

FRIDAY

BUT GOD CHOSE WHAT IS
FOOLISH IN THE WORLD TO
SHAME THE WISE,
GOD CHOSE WHAT IS WEAK IN
THE WORLD TO SHAME THE
STRONG,
GOD CHOSE WHAT IS LOW AND
DESPISED IN THE WORLD,
EVEN THINGS THAT ARE NOT, TO
BRING TO NOTHING THINGS
THAT ARE,
SO THAT NO FLESH MIGHT
BOAST IN THE PRESENCE OF
GOD.

I CORINTHIANS 1:27-29

THE HUMBLE MESSENGER

In sixteenth-century Mexico, we find the Indigenous people facing death from war, disease, and torture. They suffered particularly within their hearts. Scholars in academic halls debated whether Indigenous peoples were fully human, while holy missionaries, who saw the Native Americans' humanity, attempted to comprehensively expunge their culture with a puritanical approach to evangelization.

The Franciscans and Dominicans fought tirelessly for Indigenous rights but faced tremendous opposition. The newly appointed Franciscan bishop was almost assassinated when he stood up to the viceroy for his treatment of the Indigenous. It is in this violent and tumultuous context that Our Lady appeared to Juan Diego in 1531.

Juan Diego Cuauhtlatoatzin was an Indigenous person of low social class. He had been baptized in 1524 and took the name Juan Diego. He was also married in the Church at the same time, but his wife died five years later. Juan Diego clung to his faith and regularly walked to a mission six miles away for Mass and catechism lessons.

It was on one of these walks in December 1531 that Mary appeared to him to ask him, in the dialect of his own native language, to go to the bishop to deliver her request for a shrine to be built there. This encounter was recorded in a text called the Nican Mopohua—one of the oldest written sources on Mary's first apparition in the Americas. Juan Diego tried to deflect the mission, but she insisted, saying, "You who are my messenger . . . in you I place all of my absolute confidence . . ."

Juan Diego gathered into his *tilma*, or garment, the roses she sent as a sign. When he unfolded his tilma before the bishop, the image of the Queen of Heaven was imprinted on it, showing us how the Mother of God comes down to meet all people, even in the lowest parts of society.

What qualified Juan Diego for this mission wasn't that he was a great orator or powerful figure or respected expert. He was none of these things. He himself admitted that he was just a beginner. Mary chose him as her messenger, and in accepting, he was at once incredibly brave and amazingly humble. This opened a way for him to be part of something much bigger than he could imagine. God's plan for him was amazing.

These actions hold deep significance because this means our mother, Mary, places her deepest trust in us, too. If we say yes, we, too, can become a part of something much bigger than we can imagine. God gives the grace to be incredibly brave and amazingly humble as well. We can follow Mary to become a temple for her son, disciples and messengers of his love.

REFLECT

1. How can you grow in awareness of your littleness?
2. What are some strongholds of pride within you that the Lord is inviting you to bring to him?

_____

_____

_____

_____

_____

_____

_____

PRAY

LORD JESUS, HOW YOU LOVE ME. YOU
SURROUND ME WITH SO MANY HOLY
SAINTS. THANK YOU, LORD. THROUGH
THE INTERCESSION OF YOUR MOTHER
AND ST. JUAN DIEGO, INSTILL IN
MY HEART A BURNING DESIRE TO BE
HOLY. HELP ME TO TURN AWAY FROM
THE THINGS THAT TURN ME AWAY
FROM YOU. FORGIVE ME FOR THE
MANY TIMES I HAVE FALLEN SHORT.
RECEIVE ME AGAIN INTO YOUR LOVING
EMBRACE. YOU KNOW ME—PLEASE
ALLOW ME TO GROW CLOSER TO YOU.

SECOND WEEK OF ADVENT

SATURDAY

WHEN JESUS SAW HIS MOTHER,
AND THE DISCIPLE WHOM HE
LOVED STANDING NEAR, HE
SAID TO HIS MOTHER, "WOMAN,
BEHOLD, YOUR SON!" THEN
HE SAID TO THE DISCIPLE,
"BEHOLD, YOUR MOTHER!" AND
FROM THAT HOUR THE DISCIPLE
TOOK HER TO HIS OWN HOME.

JOHN 19:26–27

THE HOLLOW OF HER MANTLE

When we think of Mary and Advent, our minds can easily turn toward her appearance in scriptural scenes of this season: her pregnancy, her time with Joseph, her visit to Elizabeth, and of course, the nativity. These scenes remind us of how our Savior came into the world through the tenderness of a loving, joyful mother. Thirty-three years later, Jesus on the Cross entrusts Mary to the care of his disciple John, saying, "Woman, behold, your son!" We understand this to be the point at which Jesus gives Mary to all of us as a mother.

Just as she appeared to Juan Diego, she comes to us as our mother in faith. We listen to the words she spoke to him as recorded in the Nican Mopohua, trusting that she addresses us as well: "Am I not here who am your mother? Are you not under my shadow and protection? Are you not in the fold of my mantle, in the cradle of my arms?"

Juan Diego was full of apprehension and uncertainty. In speaking with the bishop, he was out of his league. At one point, he tried to avoid Mary because he felt as if he was being asked to do too much.

Mary sought him out, however, and anticipated his needs. She assured him in the language and appearance of his local culture. She gave him what he needed to fulfill her request, and the sign he carried has brought millions to deeper faith.

Mary does the same for us. She wants to bring us to her son and is uniquely positioned to help us. Let us call on her in this Advent season. She will give us what we need and more.

REFLECT

1. What gets in the way of a consistent life of faithfulness for you? What distracts you or gets you off track?
2. How can you call on Mary for her help?

PRAY

*OH LORD, THE LIGHT OF YOUR LOVE
REVEALS TO ME WHO I TRULY AM
AND THE FULLNESS OF MY IDENTITY,
NOT THE SHADOW THAT I PERCEIVE
MYSELF TO BE. IF I ONLY KNEW THE
EXTENT OF YOUR LOVE FOR ME,
I WOULD WEEP FOR JOY. IT WOULD
BE TOO MUCH FOR ME TO CONTAIN.
I WOULD SHOUT FROM THE ROOFTOPS
OF THIS LOVE. YOU GIVE ME YOUR
MOTHER TO HELP ME IN MY WEAKNESS.
I THINK TOO LITTLE OF MYSELF,
BUT SHE INVITES ME INTO THE
ADVENTURE OF PROCLAIMING YOUR
GOOD NEWS. WHEN I DOUBT YOU
OR MYSELF, GIVE ME CONFIDENCE
AND YOUR GRACE. SEND ME MARY'S
HELP AND PROTECTION.*

THIRD WEEK
OF ADVENT
THE WAY OF
ST. JOSEPH

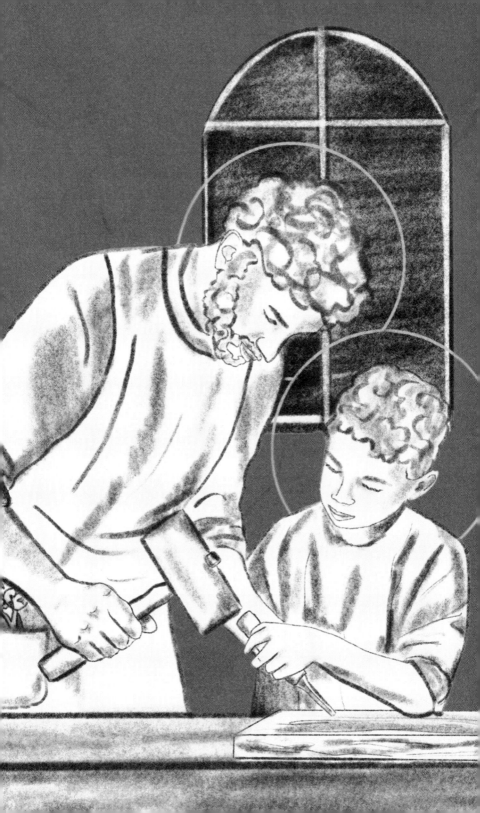

THIRD WEEK OF ADVENT

SUNDAY

SO THEN YOU ARE NO LONGER STRANGERS AND SOJOURNERS, BUT YOU ARE FELLOW CITIZENS WITH THE SAINTS AND MEMBERS OF THE HOUSEHOLD OF GOD, BUILT UPON THE FOUNDATION OF THE APOSTLES AND PROPHETS, CHRIST JESUS HIMSELF BEING THE CORNERSTONE, IN WHOM THE WHOLE STRUCTURE IS JOINED TOGETHER AND GROWS INTO A HOLY TEMPLE IN THE LORD; IN WHOM YOU ALSO ARE BUILT INTO IT FOR A DWELLING PLACE OF GOD IN THE SPIRIT.

EPHESIANS 2:19–22

ST. JOSEPH
MAKES A HOME FOR US

We know Joseph was a carpenter, but that is something of a simplification. Scripture uses the word *tekton* for his trade, meaning he was a craftsman who built homes. He would have used wood, yes, but also stone and mortar. He would have worked with other builders on projects that took time to complete, projects that would stand for years and outlive their creator.

It is easy to imagine Joseph building a home for Mary and Jesus in Nazareth, pouring a lot of care and effort into their dwelling place. He improved the structure to suit their needs and created furnishings such as beds, tables, chairs, counters, and storage spaces. He created a place where the Holy Family could share life together in Nazareth—a home.

People learned a trade such as a *tekton* through apprenticeship. They did not go to school to learn principles; they learned on the job. They began as a gofer, a low-level helper. If they watched closely and became useful, they advanced in position and responsibilities. As they were exposed to more types of projects, they were trusted to do more on their own until they had all the skill they needed to build on their own.

Apprenticeship happens mostly through imitation. Joseph, then, learned by doing. And this is a good way for us to learn as well, especially as we look to Joseph's example. The home he built in Nazareth is big enough to welcome us because we can observe his actions and dwell with the Holy Family as well.

So, in the week ahead, let's look to Joseph's actions. He was a man of deep silence. The Bible does not offer a single recorded spoken word of his, though his faithful actions speak volumes. We can think of ourselves as stepping into an apprenticeship with him not to build a structure of stone and wood but to build a space where Jesus can live within us, where we can share life with Mary.

REFLECT

1. Think of someone you admire—a close friend you look up to, a mentor who guides you, a leader who inspires you. What speaks to you in their actions? Make a list of what you observe about what they *do*.
2. How does their behavior reflect the way Jesus lived? What parts of their example do you want to emulate?

PRAY

ST. JOSEPH, ATTUNE ME TO THE POWER
OF LEARNING BY EXAMPLE. JESUS
LEARNED BY WATCHING YOU, AND I
LEARN JESUS'S WAY BY OBSERVING
HIM. OH HOLY CRAFTSMAN, HELP ME
BUILD A SUITABLE HOME IN MY HEART
FOR JESUS TO LIVE, A PLACE WHERE
MARY CAN PRAY WITH ME, A SPACE
WHERE I CAN OBSERVE YOU AT WORK.
YOU PROTECTED AND PROVIDED FOR
JESUS THE SON OF GOD AND FOR MARY
HIS MOTHER. PROTECT AND PROVIDE
FOR ME, TOO, THAT I CAN PREPARE A
PLACE WITHIN MYSELF FOR THE HOLY
FAMILY TO DWELL.

THIRD WEEK OF ADVENT

MONDAY

JECHONI'AH WAS THE FATHER OF
SHE-AL'TI-EL,
AND SHE-ALTI-EL THE FATHER OF
ZERUB'BABEL,
AND ZERUB'BABEL THE FATHER OF
ABI'UD,
AND ABIUD THE FATHER OF ELI'AKIM,
AND ELIAKIM THE FATHER OF A'ZOR,
AND A'ZOR THE FATHER OF ZA'DOK,
AND ZADOK THE FATHER OF A'CHIM,
AND ACHIM THE FATHER OF ELI'UD,
AND ELI'UD THE FATHER OF
ELEA'ZAR,
AND ELEAZAR THE FATHER OF
MATTHAN,
AND MATTHAN THE FATHER OF
JACOB,
AND JACOB THE FATHER OF JOSEPH.

MATTHEW 1:12–16

GIVING OURSELVES OVER

At the beginning of the Gospels of Matthew and Luke are two genealogies. One begins with Adam, the other with Abraham. Both draw a line through some interesting figures down to Jesus through Joseph. These lines of ancestry tell us Joseph was a righteous man who came from a family made of kings and scoundrels, of queens and adulteresses! What a comfort that Jesus's family line is . . . complicated. Each name carries a story of how God has interacted with his people. Each name is filled with triumph and failure.

What did this lineage mean to Joseph? What was his heart regarding all this? Was he afraid of repeating sins of the past?

There is a fear in the heart of every person. Fear rightly ordered is a guardian of our humanity and an occasion of courage. When it is not rightly ordered, it becomes a disposition of inadequacy—a fear of failure that affects other decisions.

Could it be that Joseph heard those voices saying, "You don't have what it takes. You are not worthy of this family"? We can hear these voices speaking to us as well. They are telling lies that weaponize the traumas and toxicity of our past. They become the excuse for staying as we are and not responding to grace. "My family was toxic," we tell ourselves. "That is why I can't pray, or why I am addicted to my phone, porn, alcohol. . . ."

I am not saying that trauma is not real. Rather, I am saying that God can work through any situation, and that our trauma need not be an impediment to what God is trying to do in our lives. In the genealogy of Jesus, we see that dysfunction was part of a greater plan and that God was able to draw good out of it.

Though at times things may seem dark, we have cause for hope. If our family lines have long been troubled, we rejoice, for the Holy Spirit has been unleashed upon the world to make us holy (Rom 5:5). The Lord promised that his Spirit will renew our hearts and will gather and reconcile people who are divided, all to allow God to dwell with us fully (*CCC* 715). We just need to give ourselves over to the Lord.

REFLECT

1. What lies do you tend to listen to? What narratives play in your head that prevent you from trusting God or hoping for transformation?
2. How can you, like St. Joseph, surrender these lies to the Lord and listen for his voice of truth and love?

PRAY

*OH JESUS, PREPARE MY HEART FOR
GREATER DEPTH AND GREATER
DEPENDENCE ON YOU. ALLOW ME TO
BE FAITHFUL TO YOUR CALLING IN
MY LIFE, TO TRUST THAT YOU WILL
GIVE ME WHAT I NEED TO FOLLOW
YOU. ALLOW ME TO BE CAUGHT UP IN
YOUR PLANS. SWEET JESUS, BRING ME
DEEPER INTO YOUR LOVE NO MATTER
WHERE IT MIGHT LEAD ME.*

THIRD WEEK OF ADVENT

TUESDAY

NOW THE BIRTH OF JESUS CHRIST
TOOK PLACE IN THIS WAY. WHEN HIS
MOTHER MARY HAD BEEN BETROTHED
TO JOSEPH, BEFORE THEY CAME
TOGETHER SHE WAS FOUND TO BE
WITH CHILD OF THE HOLY SPIRIT; AND
HER HUSBAND JOSEPH, BEING A JUST
MAN AND UNWILLING TO PUT HER TO
SHAME, RESOLVED TO SEND HER AWAY
QUIETLY. BUT AS HE CONSIDERED THIS,
BEHOLD, AN ANGEL OF THE LORD
APPEARED TO HIM IN A DREAM.

MATTHEW 1:18–20

CERTAINTY IN WHO WE ARE

Joseph was not a scholar or a political figure or an army officer. He wasn't a man of stature according to worldly standards. He wasn't a Julius Caesar or Cicero, yet he led the Son of God to grow into manhood. He led by example. He was faithful, worked hard, and humbly provided for his family.

The Bible also tells us that Joseph was a "just man" (Mt 1:19), which means that he was self-aware and knew how his actions and perceptions reflected on his family, community, and faith. He certainly would have recognized his lack of qualifications to be the foster father of the Savior of the world. He must have felt severely mismatched to the task, yet he did not let his own weakness or insecurities become an impediment to God's will. For this, all of salvation history owes him a debt of gratitude.

From the family home he built in Nazareth, Joseph shows us humility in accepting God's call, even if he was not some great man according to the world. His humility meant he knew who he was and who he was not, and that was firm ground to stand on—a foundation strong enough to help bring Jesus into the world.

His humility also meant that he didn't place limitations on what God could or couldn't do in his life. He knew that if God was asking him to help raise Jesus, God would give him what he needed to carry that task out. His humility was strengthened by faithfulness. God did the rest.

Through our baptism, we are called Christians, which means that we are anointed ones just like Jesus. We are anointed—chosen and graced—to share in Jesus's mission to bring glad tidings to the poor, to heal the brokenhearted, and to proclaim liberty to captives. It's a big task, one we cannot carry out on our own.

But with Joseph's humility we can have certainty in who we are—God's beloved children who are anointed to bring his Good News to others. No matter what we've done, where we come from, or the gifts and talents we have, that identity is true of us. And Joseph's humility proves that God doesn't need anything else to work with to do great things.

Our faith is not lived if it is not given—if we don't make it matter in some way. Experience the joy of sharing the good news that we are loved and not forsaken, forgiven and not condemned, chosen and not rejected.

REFLECT

Complete these three sentences:

Sometimes I think I'm too _____.

But I know God sees me as _____.

These are the people and practices that help reinforce the way God sees me: _____.

_____

_____

_____

_____

_____

_____

_____

_____

PRAY

LORD, YOU LOVE ME FULLY AND DEEPLY. YOU KNOW ME BETTER THAN I KNOW MYSELF. WHEN I THINK TOO MUCH OF MYSELF, YOU ARE THERE TO REMIND ME THAT ALL I AM DEPENDS UPON YOU, EVEN MY VERY LIFE. WHEN I THINK TOO LITTLE OF MYSELF, YOU RAISE ME UP WITH YOUR LOVING CARE. HELP ME MAKE THE WAY YOU SEE ME AS YOUR BELOVED CHILD MY PRIMARY IDENTITY. HELP ME TRUST YOU TO DO GREAT THINGS THROUGH ME.

THIRD WEEK OF ADVENT

WEDNESDAY

AN ANGEL OF THE LORD
APPEARED TO HIM IN A DREAM,
SAYING, "JOSEPH, SON OF
DAVID, DO NOT FEAR TO TAKE
MARY YOUR WIFE, FOR THAT
WHICH IS CONCEIVED IN HER IS
OF THE HOLY SPIRIT; SHE WILL
BEAR A SON, AND YOU SHALL
CALL HIS NAME JESUS, FOR HE
WILL SAVE HIS PEOPLE FROM
THEIR SINS."

MATTHEW 1:20–21

STRENGTH BECOMES GENTLE

Our next lesson from the school of Nazareth is that the house of the carpenter is a gentle place. We can see Joseph's gentleness in the very first moments after Jesus's birth. As Mary labored and delivered the child, the first person to hold the Savior of the world must have been Joseph. Just imagine this man with hands like hardened leather ever-so-gently holding the Word of God made flesh.

We can picture Joseph handing Jesus to Mary immediately but getting his own moments with the newborn later in the night. What did Joseph—a young, virile, righteous man in his prime—say when he held the Savior of the world in his arms? He tenderly bestowed a name on this child: Jesus, the Messiah, the anointed one, God-with-us.

Joseph's gentleness reflects the gentleness of God. This is the Creator of the universe, remember—the Lord of space and time, the one who separated the roaring sea from the towering mountains. God could have come to us in any form he chose, but he chose to come to us as a tiny, vulnerable, shivering newborn infant. He comes to us with such gentleness that his appearance calls forth from us that same kind of gentleness to receive him.

There is a way to see and meditate on this kind of gentleness if you approach a man in your life who is a father. Ask him, "What was it like, the moment you first held your child in your arms? What happened in your heart?" Look into his eyes as he composes an answer, and you will see strength become gentle.

It is difficult for us to imagine someone so powerful becoming so gentle. God, the all-powerful one, is gentle with you. Would that we would be as gentle with ourselves as God is with us! Mary and Joseph in gentleness accepted the stable with gratitude. St. Francis, at the end of his life, apologized to his body (who he called brother donkey) for not being gentler. Let us endeavor to be as gentle with ourselves as God is with our soul. If this is how he treats us, all the more should we treat others with this same joyful tenderness.

REFLECT

1. How do you experience God being personally and intimately gentle with you?
2. How can you be gentler with yourself during this Advent season? What habits or actions can you take on to be gentler with others?

PRAY

*HOW GENTLE YOU ARE WITH US, OH
GOD. YOU DON'T FORCE YOURSELF
UPON US. YOU EVEN HELP US PREPARE
TO RECEIVE YOU. THE INCREDIBLE
WORK OF MAKING OUR HEARTS
READY TO CONTAIN ALL THE LOVE
YOU HAVE FOR US IS AN EXERCISE
OF LOVING TENDERNESS. IT IS A
MIGHTY ENDEAVOR THAT OCCURS
WITH THE UTMOST GENTLENESS. MAY
I EMBRACE THIS GENTLENESS DURING
THIS ADVENT; MAY I EXPERIENCE
YOUR TENDER EMBRACE CRADLING
ME. LORD, MAY THIS GENTLENESS
TRANSFORM ME SO I CAN SHARE IT
WITH OTHERS.*

THIRD WEEK OF ADVENT

THURSDAY

AN ANGEL OF THE LORD APPEARED TO JOSEPH IN A DREAM AND SAID, "RISE, TAKE THE CHILD AND HIS MOTHER, AND FLEE TO EGYPT, AND REMAIN THERE TILL I TELL YOU; FOR HEROD IS ABOUT TO SEARCH FOR THE CHILD, TO DESTROY HIM." AND HE ROSE AND TOOK THE CHILD AND HIS MOTHER BY NIGHT, AND DEPARTED TO EGYPT.

MATTHEW 2:13–14

THE SILENT YES

Joseph has no words recorded in sacred scripture, yet his *yes* was beyond words. It went even beyond sleep. It required incredible action, incredible creativity. When Joseph said yes to marrying Mary and raising Jesus, he was not shooting from the hip. This was a man who knew what commitment was and embraced it.

We know he was chaste in his care for Mary and Jesus. He gave himself completely to them with nothing reserved for himself. This chastity generated creativity for Joseph, just like it does for us. It led him to surprising places.

I believe there is a misconception about St. Joseph. In the Middle Ages, he was depicted as an older man, as if to suggest that to protect the virginity of Our Lady, Joseph must have been older. How quickly we project our own weakness onto Joseph! No, I picture St. Joseph as strong and young. It was a young man who had something to offer, something to give when Mary (and the whole world!) needed so much.

Joseph's yes was an offering of love. At times, that yes meant he was very active in situations that were dynamic and changing rapidly; he offered himself in the journey from Nazareth to Bethlehem and gave himself further when he led the Holy Family through four hundred miles into Egypt. At other times, his yes meant that he was solid and steady, ready to embrace the monotony and faithfulness of daily life; he gave of himself when they returned to Nazareth and settled into life there as they raised Jesus.

Joseph is a good guide for us in Nazareth. He lived with two sinless people, Mary and Jesus. If anything went wrong, we can imagine who it was they looked at! Though Joseph was not perfect nor sinless, he said yes to the invitation to bring Jesus into the world. There are times when what God asks of us feels like it's too much, but we have it within us to give the same yes—to rise to Joseph's example of faithfulness.

REFLECT

1. What fears arise when you contemplate giving a full-hearted yes to God? Name them here, and ask God what to do about them.
2. If you were to thoughtfully make a yes to God with your actions, as Joseph did, what would you do?

PRAY

LORD GOD, EVERYTHING WE HAVE IS A GIFT FROM YOU. YOU SUSTAIN ME WITH LIFE, AND YOUR LOVE DRAWS ME TO YOU—EVEN HERE AND NOW IN THIS MOMENT OF REFLECTION. ALL I NEED TO DO IS SAY YES TO YOUR INVITATION TO BE LOVED, AND TO LOVE IN RETURN. YET SO MUCH MAKES ME FEARFUL! I DON'T WANT TO LOSE CONTROL OF MY LIFE. I'M AFRAID OF WHAT I'LL BE ASKED TO DO; I'M WORRIED I WON'T GET WHAT I WANT. STILL, I KNOW THAT LIFE WITH YOU DOES NOT COMPARE TO ANY LIFE I COULD BUILD ON MY OWN. GIVE ME JOSEPH'S JOYFUL AND CONFIDENT YES, AND LEAD ME WHERE YOU WILL.

THIRD WEEK OF ADVENT

FRIDAY

IN THOSE DAYS A DECREE WENT OUT FROM CAESAR AUGUSTUS THAT ALL THE WORLD SHOULD BE ENROLLED. . . . AND JOSEPH ALSO WENT UP FROM GALILEE, FROM THE CITY OF NAZARETH, TO JUDEA, TO THE CITY OF DAVID, WHICH IS CALLED BETHLEHEM, BECAUSE HE WAS OF THE HOUSE AND LINEAGE OF DAVID, TO BE ENROLLED WITH MARY HIS BETROTHED, WHO WAS WITH CHILD. AND WHILE THEY WERE THERE, THE TIME CAME FOR HER TO BE DELIVERED. AND SHE GAVE BIRTH TO HER FIRST-BORN SON AND WRAPPED HIM IN SWADDLING CLOTHES, AND LAID HIM IN A MANGER, BECAUSE THERE WAS NO PLACE FOR THEM IN THE INN.

LUKE 2:1–7

CREATIVE COURAGE

In *Patris Corde* (With a Father's Heart), Pope Francis speaks of St. Joseph's creative courage, which "emerges especially in the way we deal with difficulties. In the face of difficulty, we can either give up and walk away, or somehow engage with it. At times, difficulties bring out resources we did not even think we had."

As they prepared to leave Nazareth for their journey to Bethlehem, Joseph's creative courage was on full display. He was encouraging and resourceful.

When they arrived, he was more than likely knocking on the doors of relatives and acquaintances. He would begin, "Cousin, I am here with my wife journeying from Nazareth," only to hear, "My deepest apologies, but there is not a single inch left with the rest of the family visiting already."

Each time they were turned away, Joseph turned to Mary and offered an encouraging word. "Don't worry, Mary, Auntie Rebecca will let us in." And when they were turned away, he would cheer her by saying, "You know, there was not much room there anyway. We are going to find an even bigger place—we need a bigger room! My Auntie Rachel will let us in . . . Don't worry, we will find a bigger place!" And Mary would smile.

Then finally, when they were at last shown a stable—a cave with the odor of work animals—Joseph's creativity would find its match! On entering the cave, with great pomp and circumstance, he would make Mary laugh, saying, "Welcome, my lady, your palace awaits! Enter in, this is it! Look at all this space! And a cradle, ready-made! Good craftsmanship, if I may say so. Allow me to be your herald! Make way for the queen! Greetings, Lord Ox and Duke Donkey! So good of you to greet us. Behold, the queen is entering in! At your service, my lady! Make way for the coming of the Lord!"

Much later, Joseph died in Nazareth with Mary and Jesus at his side. Here, I imagine, his sense of humor was not diminished even as his strength was gone and his face was pale. We can imagine his same creativity appearing between coughs: "Don't worry, Mary, I'm going to find a bigger place! Allow me to be your herald." Mary, caught by surprise, laughs through her tears. Jesus responds, "Yes, in my father's house there are many rooms." And Joseph with his last breath says, "Make way for the coming of the Lord."

REFLECT

1. What are the challenges that consistently drag you down?
2. How can you learn from St. Joseph to reflect creative courage in the face of these difficulties?

_____

_____

_____

_____

_____

_____

_____

PRAY

*HEAVENLY FATHER, YOUR LOVE IS
SO CREATIVE. IT IS WHAT CREATED
THE WORLD! THERE'S NOTHING
THAT YOU CANNOT DO; ANYTHING
IS POSSIBLE WITH YOU. WHEN LIFE
THROWS OBSTACLES AT ME, I SO
OFTEN STUMBLE. ALL I CAN SEE IS THE
PROBLEM AND THE INCONVENIENCE I
FACE. HELP ME TO TAKE ON JOSEPH'S
RESILIENCE AND COURAGE. THE MORE
I LIVE IN YOUR LOVE, THE MORE HOPE
COLORS MY ATTITUDES. HELP ME
BRING YOUR JOY AND CREATIVITY TO
MY DAILY LIFE.*

85

THIRD WEEK OF ADVENT

SATURDAY

AN ANGEL OF THE LORD APPEARED
IN A DREAM TO JOSEPH IN EGYPT,
SAYING, "RISE, TAKE THE CHILD AND
HIS MOTHER, AND GO TO THE LAND
OF ISRAEL, FOR THOSE WHO SOUGHT
THE CHILD'S LIFE ARE DEAD." AND HE
ROSE AND TOOK THE CHILD AND HIS
MOTHER, AND WENT TO THE LAND OF
ISRAEL. . . . AND HE WENT AND DWELT
IN A CITY CALLED NAZARETH, THAT
WHAT WAS SPOKEN BY THE PROPHETS
MIGHT BE FULFILLED, "HE SHALL BE
CALLED A NAZARENE."

MATTHEW 2:19–23

EMBRACING THE ORDINARY

The presence of St. Joseph had many blessings for Jesus and Mary not just in times of difficulty but also in the ordinary. That's where holiness grows—in the mundane daily experience of our lives.

As a craftsman, Joseph knew the value of showing up every day. He worked on homes, which were big projects; you had to keep at it over weeks and weeks to complete a structure worthy of family life. He was a blue-collar worker who knew that steady, quiet progress added up over time. He didn't expect to achieve great things overnight.

We can imagine that Joseph taught Jesus how to carry a large beam of wood. Perhaps there was a time when Joseph was looking for a log to build a home. After felling the tree, Joseph said to Jesus, "Here, son, when you carry the log, it is best to embrace it like so, and put it on your shoulder like this, to better carry it." Could it be that, on that fate-filled Friday, Jesus heard Joseph's voice yet again when he was tasked to carry a wooden beam to Calvary?

We can see how the hidden, quiet life of Nazareth prepares us for the dramatic events in Jerusalem where Jesus suffered, died, was buried, and rose again. When we learn to find God in these everyday experiences, then we are on our way to Jerusalem, where we can join Jesus in the Cross and Resurrection. When the ordinary becomes a meeting place with God, then it also becomes a place where we can learn to love as Jesus did—totally and selflessly. It becomes a place where we can die to ourselves and find new life.

We ask the Holy Family to teach us the way of Nazareth, to guide us in learning how to have reverence for the everyday. Nazareth is, after all, where God chose to join our humanity—not in some grand revelation from heaven but in a sleepy, average town where nothing much was happening. If God can take on flesh in a place like this, God can make us holy wherever we are. We don't have to travel to the Vatican or a shrine or mountaintop to find God—from New York to Los Angeles, from Wall Street to Main Street, he shows up to meet us in our humdrum, ordinary experience.

REFLECT

1. What parts of your daily life do you find tedious? How might you be able to see in those experiences an opportunity to be selfless?
2. What kinds of things might you be able to do with God if you quietly show up every day?

_____

_____

_____

_____

_____

_____

_____

_____

PRAY

*OH, HOW I LONG FOR YOU, GOD,
KNOWING THERE IS NO TREASURE
OR BEAUTY ON EARTH THAT IS
COMPARABLE TO WHAT THE HOLY
SPIRIT IS ABLE TO CREATE WITHIN ME
DAY BY DAY—A MEETING PLACE WHERE
I CAN DELIGHT IN YOU, ALMIGHTY
ONE. GRANT ME THE FAITHFULNESS
OF JOSEPH TO APPROACH THIS INNER
SPACE WITH REVERENCE, LORD, FOR IT
IS WHERE YOU DWELL WITHIN ME. IT IS
WHERE YOU TEACH ME THE PATIENCE I
NEED TO CARRY MY CROSS.*

FOURTH WEEK
OF ADVENT
THE WAY
OF MARY

FOURTH WEEK OF ADVENT

SUNDAY

"THERE WAS A MAN SENT FROM GOD, WHOSE NAME WAS JOHN." JOHN WAS "FILLED WITH THE HOLY SPIRIT EVEN FROM HIS MOTHER'S WOMB" BY CHRIST HIMSELF, WHOM THE VIRGIN MARY HAD JUST CONCEIVED BY THE HOLY SPIRIT. MARY'S VISITATION TO ELIZABETH THUS BECAME A VISIT FROM GOD TO HIS PEOPLE.

CATECHISM OF THE CATHOLIC CHURCH 717

ALLOWING THE
LORD TO INCREASE

As the Christmas feast draws near and the busy parts of this holiday season grow noisier and more demanding, I invite you to consider Mary. This week, we will explore her stillness, her humility, her trust, her prayerfulness.

It was from Nazareth that Mary set out in haste to the hill country after hearing her cousin Elizabeth was with child. It was at their greeting that a fire passed from child to child. This same fire the Lord longs to place within you—a fire to bring those in bondage the good news of their deliverance and to cry from the wilderness, "Prepare the way of the Lord" (Lk 3:4). Pray to be consumed by this fire.

This week I invite you to enter into the prophetic nature of our Advent journey by prayer and acts of service to those in need. Let us joyfully prepare our hearts to say with St. John the Baptist once again, "He must increase, but I must decrease" (Jn 3:30). In this time when the days are still growing shorter and the nights longer, let us call out to the Lord to increase in our world, in our home, and in our hearts.

To allow the Lord to increase is to allow the light to be seen in another's darkness. It is a prophetic act to see the goodness in your neighbor when others would dismiss this as unprofitable and foolish. There is a value to the meaning we find there.

To decrease so that he might increase means, among other things, seeing the good in others and giving thanks for that. It means seeing the needs of others before your own. It means sacrificing our own likes and wants for the sake of the other. It means seeing light in the darkness. I invite you as a family or community to seek out a volunteer opportunity at a food bank, soup kitchen, or other such opportunity. Seek out the place where you can offer some service with joy! See the goodness in the brokenness. Do not go to fix a problem, but go to love those whom the Lord is sending you. Let us then decrease so that he may increase.

REFLECT

1. How can you "decrease" in this Advent season? What are the practices you can take on that will allow the Lord to increase in you and in the world?
2. How can you bring light to the darkness in your relationships and community? How can you bring goodness to brokenness?

PRAY

*OH LORD, MAY YOU INCREASE IN ME
TO HEAL, TO MEND, AND TO BRING
FREEDOM. MAY TOXIC WOUNDEDNESS,
UNGRATEFULNESS, AND MY SLAVERY TO
ANXIETY DECREASE. YOUR BLESSINGS
ARE SO GREAT—HELP ME MAKE SPACE
FOR THEM. IN HUMBLING MY HEART,
MAY I BE OPEN TO YOUR BLESSINGS.
LET ME BE CONTENT WITH LITTLE
THINGS AND EXPRESS GRATITUDE FOR
WHAT HAS BEEN GIVEN.*

FOURTH WEEK OF ADVENT

MONDAY

THE ANGEL SAID TO HER, "THE HOLY SPIRIT WILL COME UPON YOU, AND THE POWER OF THE MOST HIGH WILL OVERSHADOW YOU; THEREFORE THE CHILD TO BE BORN WILL BE CALLED HOLY, THE SON OF GOD. AND BEHOLD, YOUR KINSWOMAN ELIZABETH IN HER OLD AGE HAS ALSO CONCEIVED A SON; AND THIS IS THE SIXTH MONTH WITH HER WHO WAS CALLED BARREN. FOR WITH GOD NOTHING WILL BE IMPOSSIBLE." AND MARY SAID, "BEHOLD, I AM THE HANDMAID OF THE LORD; LET IT BE TO ME ACCORDING TO YOUR WORD."

LUKE 1:35–38

YES TO EVERY MOMENT

We would be remiss to think that Mary's yes was limited to the moment that the angel Gabriel announced to Mary that she would bear the Christ child. We would not understand what the yes really means.

Many times, our whole lives hinge on one decision. If you have been married for more than fifteen minutes, you know that the yes is not just to the flowers and the dress, the "I do" and the champagne. It requires your everything. This can be said of any vocation.

When Mary said yes as a teenager, she said it as a whole-life commitment. Her yes in this moment was not just a momentary encounter with God but a yes to be a mother, to raising the Son of God, and to all the suffering that would entail.

Like Mary, we are here to do the will of God. In his will we are free. May we be delivered from overconfidence in our own strength. May we be delivered from lacking trust in him.

If we're honest with ourselves, we will see that we are just beginners in the spiritual life. Much of our spiritual journey is this ebb and flow between us wanting to enthrone ourselves and us returning to him with repentant hearts. Some of us will grow weary of the back-and-forth, but this is a mistake. Properly speaking, that back-and-forth is the transformation of our anxiety-driven need for God into an authentic trust that is based on an authentic, well-balanced love. We are receiving every grace from on high for this transformation to occur in our souls. The threshold is our clear and firm decision to say yes to every moment as Mary did.

REFLECT

1. How is the Lord asking you to deepen your yes to him?
2. What is holding you back from making a commitment to this invitation?

PRAY

LORD, MAY MARY'S CONSTANT YES RESOUND IN MY HEART. ASSIST ME NOW WITH WHAT YOU HAVE PLACED WITHIN MY HEART. HEAL THE TIMES I HAVE TURNED AWAY, AND INTENSIFY THE DESIRE TO FOLLOW YOU WITH MY WHOLE SELF.

FOURTH WEEK OF ADVENT

TUESDAY

BUT NOW THUS SAYS THE LORD,
HE WHO CREATED YOU, O JACOB,
HE WHO FORMED YOU, O ISRAEL:
FEAR NOT, FOR I HAVE REDEEMED
    YOU;
I HAVE CALLED YOU BY NAME, YOU
    ARE MINE.
WHEN YOU PASS THROUGH THE
    WATERS I WILL BE WITH YOU;
AND THROUGH THE RIVERS, THEY
    SHALL NOT OVERWHELM YOU;
WHEN YOU WALK THROUGH FIRE YOU
    SHALL NOT BE BURNED,
AND THE FLAME SHALL NOT
    CONSUME YOU.

ISAIAH 43:1–2

TRUST LIKE MARY

Everything in our culture today pushes us away from accepting suffering. We are taught to flee from any discomfort, to distract ourselves from what is unpleasant. We try to protect our ego at any cost. Suffering arrives as an opportunity to let go of the illusion of self-reliance.

Many tests will come as we grow closer to God, but these are only occasions where our love is shown true. From these tests comes a sweet, fragrant offering. Just as the balsam tree from which incense comes must be pierced time and time again in order for the fragrant sap to come forth, so too does our faith require periods of trial and suffering to bear goodness in the world. Just as the scent of the most beautiful of flowers is only preserved by crushing the petals, so does our journey toward God require a process of breaking us down.

We need regular reminders that faith and love do not come to us without sacrifice. Mary understood this deeply when Simeon prophesied that her heart would be pierced (Lk 2:34–35). At these moments of sacrifice, she grew nearer to God for she knew that God was faithful. "He who is mighty has done great things for me," she proclaims in the uncertainty that followed the Annunciation, "and holy is his name" (Lk 1:49). She shows us how faith is more than a mere assent of our intellect—it is a complete trust in God's providence and will for our lives.

In moments of difficulty, we tend to ask, "Why is this happening?" or "Where is God right now?" We tend to turn away from God as though we've been rejected when experiencing suffering. Like Mary, we need to approach these moments as opportunities to deepen our trust in God and to call out to him in faith.

REFLECT

1. Recall a period of suffering you've experienced—a moment of grief, a rejection, a betrayal, an illness, or an injury. Write down the questions you asked of God in this experience.

2. Mary knew God's answer to sacrifice and suffering is simply "I am with you." That is not a direct answer to the questions you list here, but it is nevertheless an answer. How was God present to you in your experience of suffering, drawing you nearer to him?

PRAY

LORD JESUS, ON THE CROSS, YOU TURNED TO THE BELOVED DISCIPLE— AND TO ME—AND GAVE YOUR MOTHER TO US. ALLOW ME TO RECEIVE THE GIFT YOU OFFERED WHEN YOU SAID, "BEHOLD YOUR MOTHER." ESPECIALLY WHEN I FACE SUFFERING AND UNCERTAINTY, HELP ME TO TRUST YOU LIKE SHE DID.

FOURTH WEEK OF ADVENT

WEDNESDAY

MARY, MY DEAREST MOTHER, GIVE ME YOUR HEART SO BEAUTIFUL, SO PURE, SO IMMACULATE, YOUR HEART SO FULL OF LOVE AND HUMILITY, THAT I MAY BE ABLE TO RECEIVE JESUS IN THE BREAD OF LIFE, LOVE HIM AS YOU LOVED HIM AND SERVE HIM IN THE DISTRESSING DISGUISE OF THE POOREST OF THE POOR.

ST. TERESA OF CALCUTTA
(MOTHER TERESA)

SEEING YOURSELF
AS GOD SEES YOU

Ponder how the Lord longs to be known by you right now! Be aware, this mountain can only be ascended by the path of humility. The Word of God teaches, "Humble yourselves before the Lord and he will exalt you" (Jas 4:10). Ask Mary to teach you the true meaning of humility today.

If this fire takes hold within your heart, you will have no need to search for humiliations; they will come. We can see this easily in the life of Mary. The minute she gave her yes to God, she faced humiliation: She was a single, unmarried mother. Then, at the foot of Cross, she appeared as the mother of a man crucified as a common criminal.

We can imagine how easily we might turn away from God in the face of such suffering. We might grow prideful and forget God altogether, turning to the sin of self-reliance. Or we might grow prideful in another way: by forgetting God's *love* and seeing ourselves as unworthy of his goodness.

Mary teaches us to find the true meaning of humility: to see ourselves as God sees us. She teaches us that to follow the Lord is to walk the path of a prophet by striving to be faithful for the sake of his love. When the humiliations come, do not let your heart grow hard, but receive them as gifts. If your brother upsets you, ask first when you have done the same and rejoice that the Lord is showing you how you need to change through him. See the light in the darkness. Beware, for it is possible to endure humiliations and to grow proud. No, dear soul in search for God, humble yourself in the sight of the Lord, and he will lift you up!

REFLECT

1. What comes to your mind when you try to see yourself as God does?
2. In what ways does pride hinder you from loving God and others?

PRAY

*OH GOD, IN PRESERVING THE VIRGIN
MARY FROM EVERY STAIN OF SIN, YOU
PREPARED A DWELLING PLACE WORTHY
OF YOUR SON. PLEASE PURIFY ME
BY HER INTERCESSION THAT I MAY
PREPARE A PLACE FOR JESUS TO DWELL
IN MY HEART. GRANT ME HER HUMILITY
AND TRUST SO THAT I MAY SEE THE
LIGHT IN DARKNESS AND BE FAITHFUL
TO YOUR LOVE.*

FOURTH WEEK OF ADVENT

THURSDAY

AND IN AN INSTANT, SUDDENLY,
YOU WILL BE VISITED BY THE
LORD OF HOSTS.

ISAIAH 29:5-6

ENTERING HIS STORY

St. Francis of Assisi would spend hours in meditation, contemplating God's love. His meditation centered on the story of Jesus. The poor man of Assisi longed to make Jesus present in every aspect of his life. St. Francis embraced a gospel life, which he called a life of penance. He saw the beauty in creation and the goodness of the Incarnation. When he came upon a chapel that was unkept, he would clean with tremendous devotion the place where Holy Mass was celebrated. When the priest would elevate the host and chalice during Mass, St. Francis would bow in adoration and say, "My God and my all." He longed to go to the holy places and eventually was able to visit the very land that Jesus walked. He yearned to enter into the poverty of Jesus's birth. And now we, in our hearts and homes, have occasion to enter the story of Jesus just as St. Francis did.

We become part of God's story by doing God's work in this world. We show our family members patience, love, and commitment. We journey with the lost and accompany the grieving. We serve wherever we can, but the poor of heart and home most especially. In these acts, we become like the apostles who furthered the work of Jesus after the Crucifixion. We make his love known in the world.

This love first came into the world in the most surprising of ways: by taking on the form of a vulnerable and dependent baby. How is it that God, who is all-powerful, all-knowing, and omnipresent, could so humble himself? Yet this is what God has done. He submits himself to our criterion of understanding. That God became man means that God was a baby. What profound humility. The lover of our souls would go to any length to communicate his love for us. Let us stop running away from him in our distractions and egos. Let us run to him and enter his story.

REFLECT

1. Write down three ways you can make Jesus present in the world.
2. What distracts you from experiencing God's love?

PRAY

*LORD, HELP ME TO REMOVE
UNNECESSARY THINGS THAT OCCUPY
SPACE IN MY HEART. FILL ME WITH
YOUR PRESENCE. LOOK UPON ME WITH
YOUR LOVING GAZE SO THAT MY SOUL,
WILTED BY THE WINDS OF THE WORLD,
MAY GROW AGAIN AND BLOSSOM LIKE
THE LILY. LOOK UPON ME, LORD, AND
RESTORE ME WITH YOUR GLANCE.*

FOURTH WEEK OF ADVENT

FRIDAY

CAN A WOMAN FORGET HER
SUCKING CHILD,
THAT SHE SHOULD HAVE NO
COMPASSION ON THE SON OF
HER WOMB?
EVEN THESE MAY FORGET,
YET I WILL NOT FORGET YOU.
BEHOLD, I HAVE GRAVEN YOU
ON THE PALMS OF MY HANDS.

ISAIAH 49:15–16

THE GOOD BEYOND SIGHT

A mother's love might help us understand the love of God. When a sick child is receiving lifesaving medicine that causes more pain at the moment, does a mother not feel the pain of her child? Would a mother not take the pain, the sickness, all of it onto herself rather than see her child suffer? Yet if she did, would not another sickness come? She knows the medicine is good for the child. She sees the good beyond sight, the good that is not apparent to a child who is simply in pain.

God's love is similar in how he knows the whole of our lives and destiny. Naturally, our sights are often set on the anxieties of the day, and we can become almost obsessed with planning every detail to protect ourselves from insecurity or pain. These become moments in dire need of a deeper understanding of God's love, which sees everything at once: our past, present, and future.

Mary can teach us to follow more deeply in this way. In her complete abandonment to him, we see how to move beyond the mere beginnings of spirituality and venture into the wider field of becoming who we were created to be.

This is not simply an intellectual exercise of faith as an assent to truth. The way of faith that Mary models for us is a way that shapes our lives—our actions, our thoughts, our decisions, our relationships. It is a way of faith that rests on the conviction that God walks with us in every aspect of our lives, that he sees the good beyond our sights, and that there is nothing about us that is too insignificant for his love.

REFLECT

1. What parts of your life do you keep away from God out of shame, fear, or worry?
2. How can you bring those parts to God as one step toward abandoning your life to him?

_____

_____

_____

_____

_____

_____

_____

_____

_____

_____

_____

_____

PRAY

AT THIS TIME OF THE YEAR THERE ARE MANY THINGS FILLING OUR TIME, LORD. THERE IS AN INNER FEAR OF NOT BEING ABLE TO GET EVERYTHING DONE, AN INNER WORRY THAT WE WILL MISS SOMETHING OR SOMEONE. HELP ME NOT WORRY ABOUT THAT WHICH IS BEYOND MY POWER. HELP ME STOP TRYING TO CONTROL OUTCOMES THAT ARE BEYOND ME AND WORRYING ABOUT NONESSENTIALS. I BELIEVE YOU CAN DO SOMETHING GOOD EVEN WITH MY ANXIETY, LORD. HELP ME FOLLOW MARY'S EXAMPLE BY HAVING CLARITY ABOUT WHAT IS THE MOST IMPORTANT THING IN MY LIFE AND LIVING FOR IT.

FOURTH WEEK OF ADVENT

SATURDAY

AND ZECHARI'AH WAS TROUBLED
WHEN HE SAW HIM, AND FEAR
FELL UPON HIM. BUT THE ANGEL
SAID TO HIM, "DO NOT BE
AFRAID, ZECHARI'AH, FOR YOUR
PRAYER IS HEARD, AND YOUR
WIFE ELIZABETH WILL BEAR YOU
A SON, AND YOU SHALL CALL
HIS NAME JOHN."

LUKE 1:12–13

YAHWEH REMEMBERS

How did Mary pray? We can imagine her in prayer when the angel Gabriel visited her. What was she doing? What was she praying for? What were the yearnings of her heart moments before she was told her destiny?

We all have an intention or desire that we have prayed for over a long period of time. Perhaps there was something for which we had never prayed harder and it was not fulfilled. What happened then to our faith? There are some petitions that our hearts will not allow ourselves to stop praying. It is almost as if it is the one thing we remember. We remember the prayer so much that we even forget that we always pray for it. These are the prayers of the deepest part of ourselves. They reside within us. They are a part of our identity. Sometimes, when one of these prayers is actually fulfilled or answered, we are not sure how to pray anymore, for it has defined our prayer life.

Zechariah's name means "Yahweh remembers." He and his wife, Elizabeth, prayed for a child; that was the one prayer on their hearts. Years passed and they learned to accept that it seemed like an impossibility. But nothing is impossible for God. Then the angel Gabriel came to tell them their prayer was heard. When Gabriel addressed Zechariah, we could read his greeting like this: "Do not be afraid, Yahweh remembers." This is how God responds to our prayers—he remembers us. He remembers the one prayer you have been waiting on. Elizabeth and Zechariah prayed for a child, and God answered. This child would be the herald of the Lord.

Zechariah and Elizabeth's prayer prepared a way for the Lord. So did Mary's prayer. To pray is to remember that God remembers us, to enter into the loving union of that relationship. When the Lord visits us in that union, we receive new life. When Mary prayed, Jesus became flesh within her, and this union brought about the nativity that draws us to adore God in the manger and brings about his union with our hearts.

REFLECT

1. What have you prayed for since you were a child? How has God responded to you?
2. In what ways do you feel God has remembered you?

PRAY

*COME, HOLY SPIRIT. INCREASE MY
FAITH AND SHOW ME YOUR TRUTH.
COME TO ME NOW AND ALWAYS WHEN
I DOUBT GOD'S POWER. TEACH ME TO
PRAY WELL AND FAITHFULLY. HELP ME
TO LIVE MY FAITH BY GIVING IT TO
OTHERS THROUGH ACTS OF LOVE AND
SERVICE. REMEMBER ME, OH GOD.
PREPARE MY HEART, THAT YOU MAY BE
BORN IN ME ANEW.*

CHRISTMAS DAY

FOR TO YOU IS BORN THIS DAY
IN THE CITY OF DAVID A SAVIOR,
WHO IS CHRIST THE LORD. AND
THIS WILL BE A SIGN FOR YOU:
YOU WILL FIND A BABY WRAPPED
IN SWADDLING CLOTHS AND
LYING IN A MANGER.

LUKE 2:11–12

TIDINGS OF GREAT JOY

Today our Savior is born. Sadness should have no place on the birthday of life. No one is shut out from this joy. This is a day of great rejoicing! It doesn't matter what has happened in our past. God has become so little, so approachable, that we could hold him!

We have to approach the manger with humility. The manger is where the animals ate. How can it be that the ineffable, imminent, all-powerful, all-knowing God became so little? How can it be that the Creator of the universe was born in a cave for there was no room for him at the inn? Loving humility is the most powerful force on earth. No one can resist it. It is with this humility that we contemplate the gift of our Savior.

Let us also imagine the joy that was heard in the voice of the angel who visited the shocked shepherds: "Be not afraid; for behold, I bring you good news of a great joy" (Lk 2:10). It is almost as if at the moment Jesus was born, God told the angel to go and find someone who was still awake for this joy needed to be shared right away.

There are those in darkness even today who need to hear this message of light. These shepherds represent us. They were there, awake when everyone else was asleep. They were awake and alert to the message of the angel. Filled with joy, they ran to Bethlehem to see the infant king and to spread the Good News. So we join them, stride for stride, running to share this Good News. Today is born our Savior!

REFLECT

1. How can reflecting on the humility of God help you to grow in humility?
2. How can you humbly bring the news of great joy to those who are in darkness?

PRAY

*JOIN ME IN PRAYING THESE WORDS
FROM ST. FRANCIS IN HIS LETTER TO
THE WHOLE ORDER:*

*"LET HUMANITY KNEEL IN FEAR,
LET THE WHOLE UNIVERSE TREMBLE,
AND LET HEAVEN REJOICE WHEN
CHRIST THE SON OF THE LIVING GOD
IS ON THE ALTAR IN THE HANDS
OF THE PRIEST! O WONDERFUL
ASCENT, O STUPENDOUS DESCENT!
O SUBLIME HUMILITY! O HUMBLE
SUBLIMITY THAT THE LORD OF THE
UNIVERSE, GOD AND SON OF GOD,
SHOULD SO HUMBLY HIDE HIMSELF
FOR OUR SALVATION IN WHAT SEEMS
TO BE ONLY A SMALL PIECE OF BREAD!
LOOK, THEN, UPON THE HUMILITY OF
GOD! AND POUR OUT YOUR HEARTS
BEFORE HIM. HUMBLE YOURSELVES
THAT HE MIGHT EXALT YOU.
HOLD BACK NOTHING OF YOURSELVES
FOR YOURSELVES, THAT HE MAY
RECEIVE YOUR ALL WHO
GAVE HIS ALL TO YOU."*

FR. AGUSTINO TORRES, CFR, is a priest with the Franciscan Friars of the Renewal and the founder of Corazón Puro and Latinos por la Vida. He also serves as a retreat guide, spiritual director, and an international youth and young adult speaker.

Torres earned a bachelor's degree in art history from Seton Hall University, a bachelor's degree in sacred theology from the University of St. Thomas Aquinas in Rome, and master's degrees in divinity and theology from St. Joseph's Seminary.

Torres hosts the EWTN TV shows *ICONS* and *Clic con Corazon Puro* (in both English and Spanish). He is a cofounder of Catholic Underground, an apostolate of the Friars of the Renewal. He also cofounded the Casa Guadalupe and JPII houses of discernment. Torres is a Hispanic content contributor to Formed, host of the National Eucharistic Revival podcast *Revive*, and posts a weekly reflection on Instagram. He is on the Board of Members of the National Institute for Ministry with Young Adults, the Archdiocese of New York's Hispanic Advisory Board, and a member of the USCCB's advisory board on youth and young adults.

https://www.corazonpuro.org/
Facebook: The Community of the Franciscan Friars of the
    Renewal
Instagram: @oralecp
YouTube: Corazonpuronyc

VALERIE DELGADO is a Catholic painter, a digital artist, and the owner of Pax.Beloved. She illustrated the books *Adore* by Fr. John Burns, *Restore* by Sr. Miriam James Heidland, SOLT, and *ABC Get to Know the Saints with Me* by Caroline Perkins.

She lives in the Houston, Texas, area.

www.paxbeloved.com
Instagram: @pax.valerie

FREE *Prepare Your Heart* Companion Resources and Videos Available

Enhance your Advent experience and make it simple to customize for individual use, for use in parishes, small groups, or classroom settings with these free resources.

- weekly companion videos with Fr. Agustino Torres, CFR
- *Prepare You Heart Leader's Guide*
- *Prepare You Heart Guide for Families and Groups*
- pulpit and bulletin announcements
- downloadable flyers, posters, and digital graphics,
- and more!

THESE RESOURCES ARE ALSO AVAILABLE IN SPANISH!

Scan here to access the free resources and videos or visit
avemariapress.com/private/page/prepare-your-heart-resources.